Little Treasures

Gervase Phinn

Dalesman

First published in Great Britain 2007
by Dalesman Publishing
an imprint of
Country Publications Limited
The Water Mill, Broughton Hall,
Skipton, North Yorkshire BD23 3AG
www.dalesman.co.uk

Introductory text, poems and editorial selection
© Gervase Phinn 2007
Stories and illustrations
© the contributors 2007

ISBN 978-1-85568-244-3

Designed by Butler and Tanner Ltd
Colour origination by PPS Grasmere Limited
Printed and bound in China

PUBLISHER'S NOTE
The publisher expresses its gratitude to the children whose
stories and illustrations are reproduced in this book. Copyright is expressly
reserved on their behalf. However, given the nature of the material, it has not
been possible, despite every effort by Gervase Phinn and Country Publications
Ltd, to contact every contributor. In lieu of copyright fees,
Country Publication has made a donation to
the British Dyslexia Association.

CONTENTS

Introduction

In compiling this, the third Dalesman collection, and reading all the amusing anecdotes, insightful observations and wise words of children, I felt reassured that there are so many children out there who are such a delight: entertaining, fascinating, unpredictable, disarming and honest. We read in the papers constantly about difficult and demanding children, disaffected adolescents, teenagers high on drink and drugs, violent youngsters, the poor behaviour of pupils in schools, and we see TV programmes about uncontrollable toddlers and parents struggling to cope with their tantrums and traumas. It is easy therefore to forget that many, many children come from loving, supportive homes, and are in the hands of dedicated and enthusiastic teachers. This collection is a reminder to us all that, on the whole, children are such a source of amusement and wonder.

As with the previous two collections *Little Gems* and *Little Angels* I received so much splendid material that it has been so very hard to make the final selection. Sadly space does not allow me to include all the contributions but I would like to thank all those who submitted their stories and memories, sketches and paintings. It was kind of you to take the time and the trouble to get in touch.

Finally I shall leave you with the words of the late Malcolm Muggeridge, the television pundit and philosopher. They are taken from his autobiography *A Life* and say much better than I why children are such a delight and why we should cherish them:

'Children are the everlasting new start, life springing up again, joyous and undefiled. I know that my children must make the mistakes that I have made, commit the same sins, be tormented by the same passions, as I know that a green shoot pushing up from the earth must ripen and fall back, dead, onto the same earth – yet this does not take away from the wonder and beauty of either the children or the spring.'

Gervase Phinn
www.gervase-phinn.com

Publisher's note

Little Treasures is the final book in this trilogy of children's favourite sayings and, as with the first two books, once again we have been gratified by the submissions from members of the public – especially readers of *Dalesman* and *Down Your Way* magazines – who have shared their favourite family memories and stories. Dalesman Publishing would like to thank everyone who sent in contributions. We would also particularly like to thank all the pupils and teachers of the schools who once again have provided such splendid illustrations.

Mark Whitley, editor

Acknowledgements

The author and publishers would like to thank the pupils and staff of the following schools for their help in providing illustrations: Aston All Saints C of E Primary School, Sheffield; Cayton School, Scarborough; Christ the King RC Primary School, Thornaby, Stockton-on-Tees; Edlington Victoria Primary School, Doncaster; Grassington CE (VC) Primary School, North Yorkshire; Leamington Primary & Nursery School, Sutton-in-Ashfield; Lions Bay School, West Vancouver, Canada; Lydiate Primary School, Liverpool; Town Field Primary School, Doncaster.

The following *Dalesman* and *Down Your Way* readers have very kindly contributed to the text: Anne Austwick; Martin Bannerman; Denise Bannister; Marcia Bannister; Myra Bannister; Margaret Bardsley; Marion Barnes; R Barthram; M Beardshaw; Sheila Best; Richard Billups; Irene Bound; Barbara Bradley; Judi Brown; N Buckle; Jacqueline Buksh; Elsie Burkinshaw; Maria Butterill; Iris Calvert; Don Carson; R & D Carter; J Catherall; Beryl Caunce; Christine Charlesworth; Dorothy Corner; Gladys Crook; P D Davis; Patricia Devlin; Trevor Dorman; Harry Downham-Clarke; Barbara Dowse; Pam Duckett; Marjorie Emsley; George Evans; I Foster; Marlene Gardiner; Margaret Gee; Douglas Gibson; Gerald Gibson; Mike Glover; Jenny Greene; Margaret Griffiths; Joan Ham; Ionne Hammons; Edwin Harrison; Jenni Harrison; J Hetherington; Michael Jenkinson; Muriel Johnson; Joan Jones; Irene Lawrence; Helen Lee; Guy Wolff Litchfield; Isobel and Jack Lovie; Anne Makin; Dorothy Milburn; W Milnes; Rose Mitchell; Elsie Morpeth; Margaret Morrell; Mary Mundy; C Newmarch; John Noble; Shirley Noble; Felicity Oliver; Jean Perry; Christine Phinn; Beth Pickup; Bob Pizey; Moira Rapson; S R Ratcliffe; Christine Reasbeck; M H Robinson; Hugh Rowland; Eileen Saunby; Joan Schmann; D H Shepherd; Heather Simpkins; Annabelle Sinclair; S Slater; Margaret Smith; Alison Staniforth; Joan Stephenson; Faith Steward; A E Swindlehurst; Jane Tarver; Wyn Thompson; Mavis Thompson; Meryl Thompson; David Timmins; J M Tindall; Daphne Toombs; Mary Townroe; Jackie Waller; Miles Walsh; Delia Waterson; E Watson; Bernard Wilkinson; Douglas Wilkinson; Mavis Wilkinson; A Wilson; A F Willshaw; Daphne Wood

'People of your age are usually in a nursing home by now'

Speaking Their Minds

Children, I have found – and particularly those fortunate to have been born in Yorkshire – speak their minds, as I soon discovered when I visited my very first school in Nidderdale as a school inspector. I sat in the small reading corner to test the children's reading skills, asking one child after another to read to me from one of a selection of books I had brought with me. The choice of *The Tales of Peter Rabbit*, the children's classic by Beatrix Potter, I found to be singularly unfortunate when I asked a healthy looking young man who lived on a farm in the dale to read to me. On that bright sunny morning I came to appreciate just how shrewd, outspoken and bluntly honest children can be.

John, a serious little boy of about seven with large, penetrating blue eyes, was clearly not very enamoured with the title of the book, screwing up his face and shaking his tousled head.

'It's about rabbits, then, is it?' he grunted.

'Yes,' I replied cheerfully. 'Would you like to read a little bit of the book for me?'

'Not really,' he said, observing me blankly. 'But I reckon I've not got much choice. Miss said we've got to read to you.'

'I see.'

'She's been in a reight state this week about yer visit and been in all t' weekend purrin' that display up on t' wall, so you'd better be looking at it.'

'Really?'

'And she's marked all us books up to date and tidied her store room.'

I smiled. 'I see.'

'And she's 'ad 'er 'air done an' all.'

'Shall we start then?' I asked, before he embarked on further disclosures.

The boy read clearly and confidently but with little enthusiasm, and soon arrived at the climax of the story when poor Peter Rabbit, to escape the terrifying Mr McGregor, who was searching for him in the vegetable patch, became entangled in the gooseberry net. The frightened little creature had all but given himself up for lost and was shedding big tears.

'What a terrible thing it would be,' I said, 'if poor Peter Rabbit should be caught.'

'Yer what?' snapped the child bristling. There was a wary, resentful look in the blue eyes.

'If Mr McGregor should catch the poor little rabbit,' I told him. 'Wouldn't it be dreadful?'

'Are you havin' a laugh or summat?' the child's voice hardened. 'Rabbits! Rabbits!' he cried, scratching the tangled mop of hair in irritation. 'They're a bloody nuisance, that's what my dad says. Have you seen what rabbits do to a rape crop?' I answered that I had not. 'Rabbits wi' little cotton-wool tails and pipe-cleaner whiskers and fur as soft as velvet,' he sneered. 'I feel sorry for Mr McGregor spending all that time plantin' and waterin' and tendin' and weedin' 'is vegetables, only to ave' 'em etten by rabbits! I'll tell thee what we do if we see a rabbit on our farm.'

I should never have asked. 'What?' I enquired.

'We shoot the buggers!'

'Oh,' I mouthed feebly. 'Do you really?'

'We don't shoot ours,' interrupted a small girl who had been eavesdropping on the conversation. She had long blonde plaits and the face of an angel.

'Don't you?' I asked.

'No,' she replied sweetly. 'We gas 'em.'

Truth Will Tell

A small child was splashing poster paint
On a great grey piece of paper.
'Do you paint a picture every week?'
Asked the school inspector.

The small child shook his little head.
'Hardly ever as a rule,
But miss said we've got to paint today –
There's an important visitor in school!'

When she was four, our granddaughter climbed on my knee for a cuddle.

'Granddad,' she explained, 'do you know that Ashley's grandma has died.'

'Oh that is sad,' I said.

'No it's all right,' she told me, 'she's got another one.'

—

I had read in a magazine that rubbing the end of a cucumber on your face was good for the skin.

'What are you doing?' asked Sue, my three-year-old niece.

'It's supposed to make me beautiful,' I replied, getting to work with the vegetable. 'Is it working?'

Sue fetched a stool, stood on it and peered at my face. 'Go on,' she said. 'Keep going, keep going.'

—

I am a classroom assistant and overheard a child of eight addressing the OFSTED inspector who was busily writing, head down, in the corner of the classroom, as the teacher taught the lesson.

'Oi, mister!' he said. 'Miss likes us to listen when she's talking.'

—

My little three-year-old great-granddaughter, Eva, was lying on the floor and systematically kicking her mother's chair with her bare feet. When chastised she just carried on until her mother told her to go and sit on the stairs until she had learned to behave. After a while her mother asked her, 'Are you ready to behave yet?'

Back came the answer, 'No, not quite yet.'

—

The teacher had a large and very realistic crocodile puppet with a zipper for a mouth. When she opened the jaws, inside was a little plastic fish.

'Oh, look, children,' she said dramatically to the infants, 'that naughty crocodile has eaten a fish.' She opened wide the mouth of the creature to show the fish and, turning to a small boy, asked, 'Would you like to take the poor little fish out of the crocodile's mouth?'

'Dream on,' he replied.

—

'Granny seventy?' exclaimed Chloe, 'Gosh, but she's so active. People her age are usually in a nursing home by now.'

—

Walking to town with our grandchildren, we came across a dead hedgehog. We held an inquest and decided it had been hit by a passing car. On returning, to our surprise it had gone. Granddad, in realms of fantasy, said it had gone to the great hedgehog cemetery in the sky.

'Don't be silly, granddad,' said four-year-old James. 'Somebody's probably chucked it in a bin.'

———

The school inspector was examining the book stock in my storeroom one playtime and I, the teacher, went to the staffroom for my morning break, leaving him to it. I arrived back to find Jessica, a six year old, hands on hips, confronting the inspector with the words: 'Only miss is allowed in there, so you can come out.'

———

At the church fête, the young curate came over to have a word with me. We were chatting away about the lovely weather and the excellent turn-out when Maddie, my grandchild of seven, piped up.

'Granny, is this the boring vicar who won't stop talking when he's in church?'

'No,' replied the curate smiling widely, 'it's the other one.'

———

When asked by her mother at the school gates if she had got a harder reading book, the little girl replied sharply: 'No, I haven't if you must know, and it's not as if you always read harder reading books, is it?'

———

'Have you been naughty too, mister?'

There's No Answer to That!

I was reading the story of *The Troll and the Three Billy Goats Gruff* to a group of children in a Bradford infant school. They listened in rapt silence as I told them about the mean and ugly troll, with eyes as big as saucers, ears as sharp as knives and a nose as long as a poker, and how he waited in the darkness under the rickety-rackety bridge for unsuspecting travellers which he would gobble up. All the children, with the exception of a small British Asian girl who sat directly in front of me, listened in rapt attention, their eyes widening at the part where the troll jumped out from under the rickety-rackety bridge. Their facial expressions changed with the story and there was an audible sigh at the end when the Big Billy Goat Gruff butted the troll into the river.

The little girl sat right under my nose, expressionless – not reacting in any way at all but observing me as she might some strange exhibit in a museum showcase.

As I closed the book I asked her, 'Did you like the story?' She nodded. 'Did the troll frighten you a little bit at the beginning?' She nodded. 'And did you feel happy at the end?' She nodded. I found this pretty hard going.

Then I caught sight of the teacher at the back of the room, smiling widely. Her expression said: 'Let the inspector get out of this one.'

It was obvious that this little girl did not find it easy to communicate. She probably had just arrived from India or Pakistan, spoke little or no English and could not understood what I was saying. Perhaps she had special educational needs.

I tried again. 'Did you think the troll would gobble up the goats?' She nodded. 'Can you think of a word to describe the troll?' She nodded. I mouthed the words slowly and deliberately. 'WHAT – WORD – COMES – INTO – YOUR – HEAD – WHEN – YOU – THINK – OF – THE -TROLL?' She stared up at me without blinking. I tried again. 'AT – THE – BEGINNING – WHAT – WORD,' I tapped my forehead, 'WHAT – WORD – COMES – INTO –YOUR – HEAD?' She continued to stare. My voice rose an octave. 'WHAT – WORD – COMES – INTO –YOUR – HEAD – WHEN –YOU –THINK – OF –THE – TROLL –AT –THE – BEGINNING – OF –THE – STORY?'

After a thoughtful pause she said in a clear and confident voice: 'Well, I should say aggressive.'

Question and Answer

'And where do you go on holiday this year, Richard?'
Asked the teacher.
'We went to Mablethorpe, miss,'
The little boy replied.
'And did you go on a donkey?'
Asked the teacher.
'Oh no, Miss,'
The little boy replied,
'On the bus.'

'And what do you do when you get to a full stop?' asked the teacher.

'Get off the bus,' replied the child.

———

My husband had taken our daughter to bed and as a treat was to read her a story. A short time afterwards she came downstairs, settled herself in a chair and said, 'Daddy is asleep now, mummy.'

———

One day the children were looking at the wrinkles on my forehead and enquiring what they were. 'You get them with all the worry children cause,' I answered. 'There is one for you and one for you…'

'And one for daddy!' they shouted.

———

While employed in banking, part of my job was to visit schools and speak to the children. One morning I was keeping an appointment to see the headteacher of a primary school and was waiting outside her office when a very angry and red-faced teacher marched one of her pupils, a small boy of about nine or ten, down the corridor.

'Miss Smith will see you in a minute,' she snapped at the child, 'and she will be very very cross with you when she finds out what you have done.'

On that the little rascal came and stood next to me. Fighting back the tears, he wiped his eyes, sniffed noisily and asked me, 'Have your been naughty too then, mister?'

—

A teacher was explaining that all words beginning with the letters 'ch' always sounded the same, as in 'chin', 'chimpanzee', 'champion' and 'challenge.'

'Not always, miss,' announced a small girl.

'Yes always, Charlotte,' came the reply.

—

A succinct answer to an examination question I once set:

'What do you know about Richard the Lionheart?'

'Nowt.'

—

'There are starving kids in the world, you know,' I told Chloe, aged seven, who clearly was not keen on the contents on the plate before her and stared at the food.

'Yes, I know,' she replied pertly, 'and I'm one of them.'

—

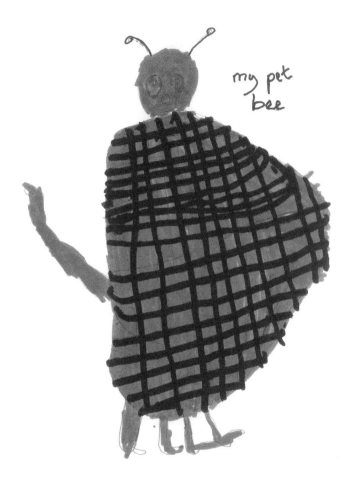

my pet
bee

My niece, Claire, was paddling in the stream fishing for tiddlers when she lost her balance and fell in.

'How did you come to fall in?' I asked her.

'I didn't, Auntie Christine,' she cried, wet through and sobbing, 'I came to catch fish.'

—

In an English literature examination paper, the candidates were asked to explain the meaning of 'bowels of the earth'. One youngster wrote, 'I don't know about the earth's bowels but I have enough trouble with my own.'

—

When my grandson was told that he had his shoes on the wrong feet, he replied, sighing, 'Don't be silly, granny, I know that they're my feet. I've always had them.'

—

My three-year-old son, having been told of the arrival of his baby sister and brought to the hospital to see her, said, 'That's no good at all! I wanted a rabbit.'

—

'Artificial insemination,' wrote one examination candidate, 'is when the farmer does it to the cow instead of the bull.'

—

It was my grandson's first day at school. His teacher asked him what his mother called him at home. Was it Nicholas, Nicky or Nick?

'She calls me cheeky monkey,' he replied.

—

Many years ago a dear friend was teaching at a school in the north of England. The other teachers noticed that a small boy always used a black crayon when drawing pictures. This went on for some time, and my friend was given the task of getting to the bottom of this mystery. Was there some deep significance with his fascination with black? Were there some profound psychological issues here? Finally she delicately questioned him why he only used the black crayon.

He replied bluntly: 'Cos that's t' only colour I've got.'

—

Out driving one day, we passed a large house and country estate. My daughter, aged six, asked who lived there.

'He's a man who races horses,' I told her.

She thought for a moment before replying, 'Oh, then he must be some runner.'

—

I was cleaning my teeth one morning when my five year old banged on the door.

'Is there anyone in there?' she asked. I, with a mouthful of toothpaste, sputtered a garbled answer.

'And is that a "Yes" or a "No"?' came a little voice from outside.

—

When my daughter was about three, I was in a multi-storey car park with her and, as I looked around for the floor number, I said, 'What floor are we on?'

With no hesitation she replied, 'A hard one.'

—

'Grandma, I'll love you till you go to your grave'

The Little Philosophers

I have met some remarkably confident, articulate and clever children in my time who have amazed me with their perceptive questions, astute comments and sharp observations.

In a junior school I met a small girl of about seven or eight, a cheerful, chattery little thing with curly red hair and a wide smile. I soon discovered that she was as bright as a button.

'Mr Phinn, are you very important?' she asked.

'No, not very,' I replied.

'Our teacher told us that you were a very important person.'

'I think she was exaggerating, just a little bit.'

'My grandpa's a very important person,' the child told me.

'Is he?'

'He wears a wig, you know, and a long red dress.'

'Does he?'

'And shiny shoes with high heels and big silver buckles on the front.'

'I see.' I had visions of a drag queen but I suspected I knew what her grandfather did for a living.

'He's a judge,' she informed me.

'Yes, I thought he might be.'

'And he locks naughty people up,' she told me. 'By the way, my first name is India and I'm named after a country.'

I leaned across the table and whispered confidentially: 'Well, my first name is Gervase and I'm named after a yoghurt.'

The child giggled. 'You're not really named after a yoghurt, are you? People aren't named after yoghurts.'

'When my mother was expecting me, India,' I told her, putting on a very serious expression, 'she had a passion for a particular French yoghurt called "Gervais", and for broccoli. I think I did pretty well with the name she picked, don't you?'

'I know what you are, Mr Phinn,' said India, giggling and pointing a little finger at me.

'Do you?'

'You're like my grandpa, Mr Phinn. You're a tease. He's a lot of fun, my grandpa.'

I bet he's not a lot of fun in the courtroom, I thought to myself, in his wig, long red dress and buckled shoes. There would be no teasing then.

'And do you like to be teased, India?'

'Yes, I do rather, it's fun. That's if it's not cruel. Grandpa says you shouldn't tease people about the way they look.

And grandpa says that we're all different and that's why the world is such a wonderful place. "Big or small, short or tall, black or white, dark or light, God loves us all." That's what grandpa says.'

'He's a very wise man, your grandpa, India,' I told her.

India sighed, shook her head and gave me a condescending look. 'Of course he is, Mr Phinn. He's a judge – and a grandpa.'

Dreaming

In the corner of the classroom,
A small child stared at the stuffed hedgehog in the
glass case.
'What are you thinking?' asked the school inspector.
'I was just wondering,' the child replied wistfully,
'What it was doing ... before it was stuffed.'

Our young son, David, a charming, impish child, had a habit of
telling you what he thought you would like to hear rather than
the dull (but truthful) facts. Confronted one day with the stark
reality that there seemed to be no escape from being caught out
in a lie, he thought long and hard and declared: 'Well, I didn't
hear my mouth say that.'

—

'I don't think our teacher knows much,' observed my grandson
after a week in school. 'All she does is ask us questions. She's a
teacher so she ought to know the answers.'

—

I asked the children to draw a picture of their favourite Bible
character. On looking at one drawing, I saw the child had
drawn a person wearing a flowing robe covered in circles.
I asked who it was. 'It's the Holy Ghost, of course,' replied the
child, 'and those circles are the holes.'

—

33

My grandson Henry was learning his cursive writing. Granddad was trying to help with the homework but Henry would much rather have been out playing football and was making very heavy weather with the writing. Finally he put down his pen with a determined gesture, looked at his granddad and said: 'I hope you live to be a hundred, granddad.'

'That's nice, Henry,' replied granddad, rather moved. 'I hope so too.'

'Yes,' Henry added, 'and then you will get a letter from the Queen and we will be able to see what *her* handwriting is like.'

———

Our grandson, aged five, had just learned to write his name. 'Look, grandma. I've written "James".' He had, but there were two letter As.

I mentioned that one was cockeyed and added, 'And you've put two As instead of one.'

He heaved a great sigh and said scathingly, 'Oh, for goodness sake, grandma.' Then, pointing to the odd one, he told me, 'Can't you see that that one's broke?'

———

Joseph, my grandson, came and sat next to me on the settee, put his arms around me and, giving me a cuddle, said, 'Grandma, I will love you till you go to your grave,' to which I replied, 'That's lovely, and will you put flowers on my grave for me?'

He looked at me and said, 'Yes, of course. And I'll turn them upside down so you can smell them.'

———

An observation by my four-year-old granddaughter, Ruby. 'Granddad, your hair is sticking up like a shark's dorsal fin.'

———

I was complaining one day about all the holes in the back lane on the way to school. My grandson replied, 'But grandma, the holes are supposed to be there. The rain needs somewhere to put its puddles.'

—

After a visit to a farmyard, my four-year-old niece was fascinated by the cows walking up the road.

'Aren't cows clever,' she remarked. 'They can walk and wee at the same time.'

—

Nicola was three when this logical interrogation took place:

Nicola: 'Grandma, were you once a girl?'

Grandma: 'Yes.'

Nicola: 'Grandma, were you once a little girl?'

Grandma: 'Yes.'

Nicola: 'Grandma, were you once a baby?'

Grandma: 'Yes.'

Nicola: 'Grandma, did you have a mummy and daddy?'

Grandma: 'Yes'.

Nicola (quite perturbed): 'Then why did they decide to call you "Grandma?" Grandmas are supposed to be old.'

—

My granddaughter asked me how old I was.

'Oh, very very old,' I told her.

'But how old?' she persisted.

'As old as my hair.'

'Well grandpa can't be very old then. He's got no hair,' she said.

—

On a country walk in the Lake District, Arthur was taken short and had to retreat into some bushes. Gillian, his little daughter, continued walking with us. Shortly after it began to rain and someone joked with Gillian, 'Aw, Gill, why have you made it rain?'

'It wasn't me,' retorted Gillian. 'It's God. He saw my dad having a wee, so He thought He would have one Himself.'

—

When our grandson was aged six, he came on one of his visits and we were sitting on a bench in the garden. As he looked up into the sky he saw a plane go into a large cloud. It seemed to take quite some time before it finally emerged. Before it did he called out to me, 'Granddad, has it got stuck in t' middle or summat?'

—

'Mum, is it the olden days now?' asked Andrew, aged five.

'No why?'

'What a pity,' he said thoughtfully. 'When I grow up and have kids, I can't tell them stories about the olden days.'

—

My son, Dominic, aged six, the little philosopher, often shares his opinions with us. One memorable statement was: 'It's a pity, granddad, that you won't be around for my twenty-first birthday party.'

—

Me: 'What's your knee for?'
Son (aged four): 'A crease in your leg.'

—

'He's not my dad – he's my mum's boyfriend'

Oh the Embarrassment!

I think every parent and every teacher has been put in the situation when children have said something which has caused us deep embarrassment.

I had just finished taking the assembly in a junior school in Scarborough, having told the children about the old Viking route known as The Lyke Wake Walk. Legend has it that the Vikings carried the 'lyke' or corpse across the bleak moors to the sea, where the body was given up to the waves.

'Well, I hope you all enjoyed that,' I said cheerfully when I had finished. The children and their teachers nodded. 'Are there any questions?' I looked across a sea of silent children. 'Anything at all?'

'Come along now, children,' came the headteacher's voice from the back of the hall. 'I'm sure there are lots of things you would like to ask Mr Phinn.'

A young frizzy-haired infant with a pale, earnest face raised a hand.

'Ah, there's someone,' I cried, relieved that at least one child had found the story sufficiently interesting to ask a question. 'Yes, and what would you like to ask?'

'What's a condom?'

'Pardon?' I jumped up as if I had been poked with a cattle prod.

'A condom? What's a condom?' repeated the child. I was completely lost for words.

'Well, it's…' I began, looking appealingly towards the teachers.

'It's a snake,' snapped the headteacher quickly.

'No, that's an anaconda, miss,' volunteered a young, helpful, red-headed boy in the senior class.

'It's a bird,' announced a teacher with great assurance.

'Condor,' exclaimed the child at the back. 'You're thinking of a condor, miss.'

The little boy, entirely undeterred, continued with the grilling. 'But what *is* a condom?'

'It's something you will learn about when you are older,' replied the headteacher firmly.

'Is it a rude word, miss?' asked the innocent.

'No, it's not a rude word, John.'

'Can I call somebody a condom then, miss?'

'No! You certainly cannot!' she snapped.

'Somebody called me a condom, miss,' the infant told the teacher.

'Well, they shouldn't have,' said the headteacher. 'Ignore them.'

'Does it begin with a curly 'C' or a kicking 'K'?' asked a fresh-faced little girl at the front.

'A curly 'C', Sarah, but–' replied the headteacher.

'And is it spelt C-O-N-D-O-M?' she asked, articulating every letter slowly and deliberately.

The frizzy-haired child continued to persevere and still had his hand in the air.

'Right, children,' the headteacher told them loudly. 'Put down your hand now, John. Everyone sit up straight, look this way, arms folded, and when we are ready we can return to our classrooms.'

When the time came for me to leave, I paused at the gate of the small school to marvel at the panoramic view which stretched out before me but was brought out of my reverie by the sound of voices. Out of sight, behind the craggy stone wall which enclosed the school, I observed three or four young boys gathered around the red-haired pupil who had tried to put his teachers right about what a condom was. He was explaining to his fascinated companions that 'You can get them in different sizes, different colours, different flavours…'

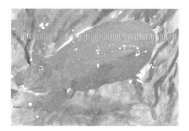

The Inspector Calls

'This work looks most impressive,' the school inspector said,
'So accurate, well-written and so neat.'
'It should be,' said the pupil shaking her little head,
'We've been practising this worksheet for a week.'

There were so many children in Sunday school that the youngest ones had to sit on the wooden floor. A five-year-old boy arrived one Sunday clutching a large family Bible.

'Surely you can't read that, can you?' asked his teacher.

'Nay, I can't read it,' he said. 'I've brought it so I won't get splinters in me bum.'

—

Some years ago I was taking a class and telling the children about Pentecost: 'The disciples were together in a locked and shuttered room when a rushing mighty wind came upon them.'

I asked the children what they would have felt like had they been there. One little lad quickly said: 'I'd have felt like holding my nose 'cos when my granddad lets off wind it smells something terrible.'

—

My four-year-old daughter, in that loud and resonating voice that small children have, announced that she had been 'making cock-porn at school'. Concerned enquiries revealed she had been making 'popcorn'.

—

44

My wife and I were spending a quiet weekend at a guesthouse in the Yorkshire Dales when, one evening, a small boy entered the lounge and asked if he could have the television on. He had arrived with a young couple, one of whom was a young man who was sitting in the corner of the lounge reading his newspaper.

'You will have to ask your dad,' I told the child, looking over to the young man in the corner.

'Oh, he's not my dad,' replied the child, 'he's my mother's boyfriend.'

Everyone stifled a laugh as the young man buried his face in the newspaper.

—

I was telling the children in my class about how important water was in our life and how we should do everything to conserve it. I asked them to list the things they could do to conserve this precious commodity. Stop the tap dripping, don't wash the car too often, ban the hosepipe were all suggested. One boy's hand suddenly shot up. 'Miss, you could do what my dad and mum do. They have a bath together.'

—

A child in my class asked me what the word 'dowdy' meant. I was very impressed and asked her where she had come across the word. She told me, 'My mummy says that you wear dowdy clothes.' I was tempted to tell the child's mother on parents' evening what her daughter had said but resisted the temptation and saved the poor woman the embarrassment. I did, however, decide to brighten up my outfits after that.

—

I was in a busy café when a lady came to the next table with her grandson, aged about three or four. When they were leaving, the little boy remained at the table until his grandmother told him to 'hurry up darling and come along'.

The café was unusually quiet when his voice filled the room.

'Here you are, grandma,' he cried, holding up two small handfuls of sachets of sugar and sauces, 'Don't forget to put these in your handbag like you always do.'

—

My two sons, one six and the other eight, watched with interest as a very large woman in front of us negotiated the stairs in the Tube station. Callum, the younger, said in a loud voice, 'Isn't that lady fat, mummy?'

His elder brother, in an even louder voice, told him off. 'You shouldn't say that – it's very rude.' Then he added. 'You should say "obese".'

—

When I was three, the story goes that the local priest called. My mother came to get me, saying, 'Come and see Father Comerford.'

My reply was, 'I'd rather see Father Christmas.'

—

When I was eight years old, my parents were having a party. My sister, brother and I were usually allowed to say hello to everybody before going off to bed. I said in front of a fair crowd of people that it wasn't much of a party without balloons. My father said that we didn't have any, to which I replied: 'Well, there are loads of balloons in the bottom drawer of mummy's dressing table.' I remember being whisked out of the room very quickly.

—

46

My small daughter asked my friend: 'Why don't you get a bra for your bottom?'

—

At a WI market stall, an elderly gentleman was selling seeds, shrubs and assorted plants. I was with my small grand-daughter, Cecile.

'You plant the seeds,' the man explained to her, 'and then, when they appear, prick out.'

Cecile let out a great 'Aaaaahhhh!' and added 'that's a very very rude word.'

—

I breast-fed both my children. We were in church for the christening of our second child and I was wearing a lovely white silk blouse. When there was a lull in the service my daughter Olivia, aged seven, said in a very loud whisper which echoed around the church, 'Mummy, mummy, you're leaking.'

—

My grandson Anthony was telling me what he had done over the weekend. 'Well, I had a bad cough and went downstairs to get a drink of water in the middle of the night, and – do you know what, granddad? – I found mummy and daddy sunbathing in front of the gas fire.'

—

My grandson, William, and I were on a bus going into Doncaster. A young man got on with a bright T-shirt across the front of which were emblazoned the letters FCUK. William looked at the T-shirt and pondered for a moment before telling me (and the other passengers): 'They've spelt it wrong, granny.'

—

Some years ago we took our fifteen year old daughter and four of her friends, all girls, on holiday to Wales. We had hired a cottage for the week, and our daughter and friends, being the age they were, did not want to come with us when we went out so we left them behind at the cottage, which had a nice garden at the rear. With the weather being very nice and sunny, they took advantage of the garden to sunbathe and play their radio. The garden backed onto the garden and house of the man who was the caretaker for our cottage. On the day we were leaving I had to take the key back to him. I knocked on the door of his house and when he answered he had his small four-year-old daughter with him. As I handed him the key, his daughter said, 'My daddy said he will be glad to see the back of you lot.'

—

On a crowded bus the passengers burst into spontaneous laughter when the small girl asked her mother in a very, very loud voice: 'Mummy, what does "bollocks" mean?'

—

My young son, looking at the elegant woman in front of us in the queue, said in a loud voice: 'I think the woman in front must have had plastic surgery.'

—

On the beach little Maisie, aged four, found a condom in a rock pool and, scooping it up in her spade, came to show us.

'Look what I've found, mummy,' she cried. 'Is it a fish?'

Quick as a flash my ten-year-old son Eric informed her, 'No, it's a contraceptive and you should use one for safe sex.'

—

I had taken my class to see HRH Princess Diana when she came to visit our town. Each child was given a small Union Jack to wave and some had brought flowers from home to give to the princess. She smiled at and chatted to the children lining the street receiving their bouquets, which she passed to a lady-in-waiting. She noticed a small boy (he was not in my class but had edged to the front and was standing with us) who was holding a rather pathetic bunch of wilting flowers. I am sure Princess Di warmed to the child, for she came over and took the flowers from him and smiled.

'And have you had the day off school to come and see me?' she asked him sweetly, at the same time ruffling the child's hair.

'No,' he replied, 'I'm off with nits.'

'A murder for my daddy and a lover for my mummy'

Out of the Mouths ...

'This morning we have a very special visitor in school,' the teacher told her class of seven year olds and gesturing in my direction. I was undertaking a short inspection in a small village school in the heart of the Yorkshire Dales one cold November day. 'And his name is Mr Phinn,' she continued. 'Mr Phinn is just in time to join us for "News time". The teacher turned in my direction. 'Every Monday morning, Mr Phinn,' she explained, 'I ask certain of the children to come out to the front of the classroom to tell us what interesting things they have been doing over the weekend. Do take a seat, Mr Phinn, and then we can begin.'

The first child to speak was a large girl with a pale moon face, large owl eyes and two big bunches of thick straw-coloured hair tied with crimson ribbons.

'An 'edgehog come out from t' bushes last night,' she announced volubly. 'And then it went back in.'

'That is unusual,' remarked the teacher. 'Isn't that unusual, Mr Phinn?'

'Yes, indeed,' I agreed. 'Very unusual.'

'Hedgehogs usually sleep all winter,' said the teacher. 'Did you disturb it, Melody?'

'No, miss,' replied the child. 'It just come out and went back in. We put some bread and milk out for it.'

'Well so long as you didn't poke it and wake it up. Let's have Duane out to the front.' The next young newsgiver was a bespectacled little boy with black hair slicked back and with a neat parting down one side. 'Now, Duane, did anything interesting happen to you at the weekend?'

'Some white worms come out of my bottom, miss,' the boy informed her.

The teacher squeezed her eyes together like someone wincing at an inward pain. 'I really don't think we want to hear about the white worms thank you very much, Duane.'

The child continued regardless. 'My mum went to the chemist to get this pink medicine which tasted like strawberry milkshake to stop these white worms coming out of my bottom.'

The teacher held up a hand as if stopping traffic. 'I think we have heard quite enough about the white worms,' she interrupted. 'Haven't we, Mr Phinn?'

'Yes, indeed,' I replied, attempting not to smile.

'I shall write the word "hibernation" on the blackboard,' announced the teacher, a red nervous rash creeping up her neck, 'and we shall talk about the hedgehog that Melody found in her garden. I am not at all certain, however, that it is a very good idea to give hedgehogs bread and milk, is it Mr Phinn?'

'No,' I agreed. 'It makes their stomachs swell and it is bad for them.'

'Actually,' said the teacher, 'I am not sure what hedgehogs eat. Do you know, Mr Phinn?'

'Yes,' I replied, and then added without a trace of a smile, 'It's worms.'

Home

In the Home Corner,
In an infant school classroom,
A boy and girl,
Rising five,
Were arguing,
Stabbing the air with small fingers,
Jutting out their chins,
And stamping little feet.
'Oh, do shut up!'
'No, you shut up!'
'I'm sick of you!'
'I'm sick of you!'
'Oh, just be quiet!'
'No, you be quiet!'
'Oh, do shut up!'
'No, you shut up!'
'What is all this?' the teacher cried.
'Were playing mums and dads,'
The infants both replied.

My granddaughter was fascinated with the dolls in a toyshop.
There were pretty authentic boy and girl dolls. 'Look, granny, at
this one,' she said, picking up the boy doll and scrutinising the
lower regions. 'That's a funny place to have a finger.'

—

My father, whose name was Harry Wood, ran a toy and cycle shop. Every 11-Plus exam time, children were promised a present if they passed to go to grammar school. One young boy had been promised a bicycle, his dream. Luckily he passed and that night on receiving his coveted award he said his prayers aloud as he always did, but his excitement took over and he said, 'Our Father who art in Heaven, Harry Wood be thy name.'

—

On Armistice Day my daughter was in a shop with her son, aged six, when a gun was fired for the start of the two-minute silence. The little lad was intrigued why everyone around him stood still, heads bent. He asked his mother what was happening and she explained that they were saying a silent prayer for all the people who had been killed in the world wars. When the gun was fired again at the end of the silence, he asked: 'Have they shot another one?'

—

Three-year-old daughter, sat in child seat in the back of the car, with mother (me) driving:
Louise: 'Mummee...'
Mummy: 'Yes, dear?'
Louise: 'Why do all the men that you know have the same name?'
Puzzled expression from mummy. 'What do you mean, dear?'
Louise: 'They are all called Dick.'
Oh dear. I have since become a much less aggressive driver.

—

I used to work in a library and every Saturday morning a little boy came in, asking for 'A murder for my daddy and a lover for my mummy'.

—

My five year olds were acting out a famous children's story. A dour little boy was the wolf in bed, disguised as grand-mamma, awaiting the visit of Little Red Riding Hood. His interpretation of the knock at the door and the instruction to 'Lift the latch, my dear, and come in' was typically Yorkshire: 'Cum in an' shut t' dooer – there's a reight draft in 'ere.'

—

My four-year-old granddaughter and I had been enjoying several games of Snakes and Ladders. She followed me into my bedroom and heard me mutter to myself, 'Drat! I've got a ladder in my tights.' At this point she dashed into the kitchen calling, 'Mummy! Mummy! Granny's got a snake in her stocking!'

—

We were attending my grandson's nativity play. The angelic little boy playing Joseph had been perfect until the end, when all the children assembled on stage to sing the final number, 'The Little Drummer Boy'. Three boys stood immediately behind Joseph with large drums, which they proceeded to bang with great gusto. I could see little Joseph getting increasingly agitated by the noise. Finally he turned to the drummers and exclaimed very loudly:

'Will you SHUT UP! You're doing mi 'ead in!'

—

Georgina, the granddaughter of a good friend of mine, aged about two and a half, was given a whole orange, peeled by her mother. Georgie, as she was known in the family, gazed at it with some disdain and lisped 'Thkin off.' Her mother, with commendable patience and a teacher's instinct to explain, said, 'No Georgie, mummy has taken the skin off already. That white stuff is called pith.'

Georgina's reply was succinct and wholly logical. 'Pith off,' she said sweetly.

———

Hayley, my three-year-old granddaughter, came into the bathroom just in time to see me remove my false teeth.

'Jeremy, Jeremy!' she screamed to her brother. 'Come quickly, nana is doing magic.'

———

Four similar-aged elderly ladies were guests at a friend's silver wedding lunch. Her three-year-old grandson burst in, then stopped in amazement. 'Daddy, daddy, come and look, there are four grandmas all together.'

———

Our granddaughter, Hannah, at the age of five, was absorbed in watching granddad shaving and removing his dentures, astonished to see he had 'toy teeth'.

———

I tried desperately to suppress my laughter when a child in my class informed me that his baby brother was to go into hospital to 'have an operation on his willy'. He continued that he was 'to have it circus sized'.

———

Child (very loudly) to parent, as the train sped through Doncaster Station: 'That virgin can't half shift.'

———

Overheard in the playground during the build-up to a school inspection: 'We've got to be good next week and work hard. Those "Odd Egg Inspectors" will be in school watching us.'

———

I was out walking with my five-year-old granddaughter Lucy. It was a perfect day – sunny with a beautiful blue sky.

'Isn't it a lovely sky,' said Lucy. 'But I wonder what it's like in heaven?'

'I don't know,' I said.

'No,' she replied, 'but it won't be long before you find out, will it?'

64

'Why has daddy got a pocket in his underpants?'

Those Tricky Questions

A teacher in a junior school was stressing the importance of safety in the home, in school and on the streets, and the children in her class were sharing their experiences. I was sitting in on the lesson.

'David, what about your accident?' asked the teacher, looking at a small boy near the front.

'Miss, I swallowed a marble,' said the boy.

'Good gracious!' exclaimed the teacher. 'That was a very silly thing to do and could have been very dangerous. You could have choked to death, couldn't he, Mr Phinn?'

'Yes, indeed,' I said.

'Miss, I was pretending it was a sweet,' continued the boy,

'and I popped it in my mouth and swallowed it by mistake. I started to cough and my mum had to smash me on the back really really hard and -'

'I think a better phrase to use would be "strike firmly" or "slap heavily", David,' interrupted the teacher.

'So, my mum had to strike me firmly on the back but it wouldn't come up, so I had to go to hospital. The doctor gave my mum this paper to get some medicine…'

'Prescription,' interposed the teacher.

'… gave mum this prescription to get some medicine and it was thick and pink and was really gross and —'

'Tasted unpleasant,' prompted the teacher.

'And it came in a big brown bottle and I had to take it for a couple of days and then one morning I was sitting on the toilet and there was a clunk and I shouted down the stairs "I've got my marble back!" and my dad said "Leave it alone!" and –'

'My goodness, David,' said the teacher hurriedly, 'what a to-do. I think we've heard quite enough about your unfortunate accident, haven't we, Mr Phinn?'

'Yes,' I said, wishing that the teacher would not constantly keep referring to me for an opinion…

I Only Asked

On Sunday, Dominic asked his dad:
'Which is the brightest star?'
'Ask your mum,' his dad replied,
'I have to clear the car.'

On Monday Dominic asked his mum:
'What's a carburettor?'
'Ask your dad,' his mum replied,
'I have to post this letter.'

On Tuesday Dominic asked his dad:
'What's a UFO?'
'Ask your mum,' his dad replied,
'The grass, it needs a mow.'

On Wednesday Dominic asked his mum:
'Which is the deepest sea?'
'Ask your dad,' his mum replied,
'I'm busy making the tea.'

On Thursday Dominic asked his dad:
'How tall are kangaroos?'
'Ask your mum,' his dad replied,
'I'm listening to the news.'

On Friday Dominic asked his mum:
'Do all kings have a crown?'
'Ask your dad,' his mum replied,
'I'm going into town.'

On Saturday Dominic asked them both:
'Do you mind me asking things,
About stars and cars and life on Mars
And kangaroos and kings?'

'Of course we don't,' his dad replied,
'Ask questions as you grow.'
'By asking things,' his mother cried,
That's how you get to know.'
Little Dominic stretched his head,
And simply answered, 'Oh.'

Six-year-old James was so excited as he had been chosen to take part in the school nativity play.

'Why can't we have Christmas every day?' he asked.

—

Four-year-old Sarah asked this question from the back of the car: 'Mummy, why are there more idiots on the road when daddy's driving?'

—

69

The new neighbours had moved in, and very soon there was a knock on the door and there stood a little girl with her bicycle.

'Have you any children?' she asked my seventy-five-year-old husband.

'I have but they've gone away,' I told her.

'Why?' she asked. 'Didn't they like you?'

—

Coming from church on Sunday, four-year-old Mark asked me: 'Mum, why does the vicar get dressed up and tell lies?'

'I don't think he does, love,' I replied.

'Oh, he does every week.'

'Why do you think that the vicar tells lies?' I asked bemused.

'Well, every Sunday he gets dressed up with his cape, puts out his hands and says "The Lord is here." Well, I've never see Him.'

—

When I was five I watched in amazement one day as grandma took out her teeth to clean them. Leaning further through the bathroom door I whispered, 'You won't be taking your eyes out, will you grandma?'

—

My young daughter was helping me hang the washing on the line when she asked: 'Mummy, why has daddy got a pocket in his underpants?'

—

'Granddad,' asked three-year-old Paul, staring at my husband's bald and shiny pate, 'how old were you when your hair slipped?'

—

When he was a youngster, my son Richard (now aged thirty and a successful accountant) was constantly asking questions: 'Why are holes empty?' 'Why are bananas bent?' 'What is the point of toes?' 'Why are oranges orange?' 'Are stars hot?' The questions were endless and I attempted to answer them as best I could. Then came the day when he asked me, 'How do people make babies?'

'I'll get your father,' I told him.

—

When my son was a toddler with enough language to start asking probing questions, he suddenly said one day, 'When I was born, did you pull my pants down to see if I was a boy or a girl?'

—

My daughter, her husband and their two little girls were having a short holiday with us. They had been out for a Sunday morning drive and unfortunately were late getting home for lunch, which was unacceptable for grandma. Halfway through lunch one of the girls said, 'Mummy, when will we be going in the doghouse?'

'I know why we have Christmas – to Sellotape Jesus'

Getting to Grips with the Language

I was just about to enter the main door of an infant school when a very distressed-looking little girl of about five or six, her face wet with weeping and her cheeks smeared where little hands had tried to wipe away the tears, tugged at my jacket.

'They've all got big sticks,' she wailed piteously.

'Who's got big sticks?' I asked, surprised.

'All on 'em. They've all got big sticks!'

'Well, they shouldn't have big sticks,' I replied.

'I want a big stick,' she cried, sniffing and sobbing, her little body shaking in anguish.

'No, you can't have a big stick. It's very dangerous,' I told her.

'I want a big stick,' she cried. 'I want a big stick.'

'You could hurt somebody with a big stick,' I said.

'But they've all got big sticks,' she howled again. 'They've all got 'em.'

At this point the headteacher appeared from the direction of the playground.

'Whatever is it, Maxine?' she asked, gently pulling the little body towards her like a hen might comfort a chick. She then looked at me. 'It's Mr Phinn, the school inspector, isn't it?'

'Yes,' I replied.

'I'm relieved about that. We have to be so careful these days. The playground supervisor came rushing into the school saying there was a strange man talking to the children.'

I suddenly felt acutely embarrassed.

'Of course, I'm so sorry. I should have come directly to the school office. It's just that this little girl was so distressed and came running up to me.' The child in question was nuzzling up to the teacher, sniffling and snuffling softly.

The small child continued to clutch the headteacher, and began to moan and groan again pitifully. 'I want a big stick, miss,' she moaned. 'They've all got big sticks.'

'Of course, you can have one,' the headteacher replied, wiping away the little girl's tears. 'You weren't there when I gave everybody one. You don't think I'd leave you out, Maxine, do you? You come with me and I'll get you a nice big one. How about that? I won't be a moment, Mr Phinn.'

'A big stick?' I murmured. 'You're giving this little girl a big stick?'

The headteacher gave a huge grin before replying, 'She means a biscuit.'

Lizzie's Road

Little Lizzie drew a long, long road
That curled across the paper like a strange, exotic snake.
She decorated it in darkest reds and brightest blues,
Gleaming golds and glittering greens.
Mum asked, 'Why all these wonderful colours?'
'Those are the rubies and emeralds and pearls,'
Lizzie explained.
'The diamonds and opals and precious stones.'
'What a wonderful road,' said mum. 'Is it magic?'
'No,' explained the child, 'It's just a jewel carriageway.'

My granddaughter, a pupil at a Roman Catholic primary school, informed me that she had been 'learning about the Immaculate Contraption'.

—

In my final year at junior school, the class of eleven year olds gave a very ambitious shadow-puppet performance to parents based on the 'Willow Pattern Plate Story'. The tension was building up in the script and the excitement grew as we reached the part where the young couple were preparing 'to flee'. The narrator, in her over-enthusiasm, inadvertently read the script as, 'Even as we speak the young couple are preparing toffee'.

—

fun

My two-and-a-half year old daughter, Jane, was being carried on her father's shoulders through Sheffield meat market when we passed a meat stall. On it was a rabbit, complete with fur, which was gutted down the front.

Jane exclaimed: 'Oh look, daddy – a pussy undone.'

———

A pupil, asked to explain the meanings of certain words, wrote: 'Erudite is a kind of glue.'

———

'Why didn't they have clothes for the baby Jesus, mummy?'

'Oh, they did. There were some lovely things to wrap him up in.'

'No there weren't, because we've learnt at school he was in a manger rude and bare.'

———

When we lived in America my daughter, Carole, aged four, attended the pre-school. Picking her up one day, I asked if she had been doing anything interesting in class that day. She told me she had learnt a new poem.

'Oh and what was that?' I asked.

'I'm a pleasant nuisance to the flag of America,' she replied.

She had been learning the Pledge of Allegiance.

———

After my four-year-old daughter had been at school for a week, I asked her how she liked being at big school.

'It's good but I haven't had my Bounty Bar yet,' she replied. I asked her what she meant and she explained: 'Well, every day before dinner, sir says, "We thank you Lord for our bounty" but nobody has given me mine yet.'

———

Whilst perusing the menu of the Chinese take-away, seven-year-old Anna announced: 'I'd like atomic crispy duck, please.'

—

On being asked to describe any pets they had, one child wrote, 'We have a dog at home. It is a library door.'

—

Discussing different types of animals, I asked the children what we call an animal that sleeps all day and comes out at night, the word beginning with the letter 'N'.

'Knackered,' came a reply.

—

Natasha, aged five, came home from school and announced to her daddy, 'Daddy, Emma weed in class today.'

'Oh dear,' replied her daddy. 'Did she have an accident?'

'No,' said Emma very indignantly, 'she weed a book.'

—

I tried to explain that at Christmas we celebrate the birthday of Jesus, and we only celebrate birthdays once a year.

A few days later one of his teachers told me James had been misleading her pupils. She explained that, the day after my conversation with James, he had arrived at school full of himself.

'Miss, miss, I know why we have Christmas – to Sellotape Jesus.'

—

The small boy told his teacher: 'My mummy and daddy were both students at university and they fell in love at the degradation ball.'

—

80

A class of six year olds had been discussing how vital water is, and how to reduce wastage. This led on to toilets and Peter piped up, "My granddad served in the sewers." The teacher thought this sounded like a good idea for a class visit or a talk to the class, so she asked his mum, who was mystified. She then realized that his granddad had been called up in 1956 and served in the Suez crisis.

—

I had been reading the story of the Nativity to an infant class, and was asking questions afterwards. 'Now class, what job had Joseph?' I asked.

One child put his hand up immediately: 'Miss, he did what my dad does. He's a carpet-fitter.'

—

Children in class were asked if anyone knew what a young rabbit was called. Bobby piped up, 'Is it a bunion?'

—

Alexander announced he had 'lost his sweating shirt' after taking it off in the playground because he was too hot. He also said, when he had a cold, that 'My nose is all blocked up and I keep bless-you-ing'.

—

My son rang me one day to ask if I could do some babysitting. Our four-year-old grandson was listening to the conversation and he called out, 'I'm not a baby, and I don't want to be sitted on.'

—

When I explained to an eight year old in my class, who complained of a headache, that teachers were not allowed to give children aspirin, he thought for a moment and asked: 'Then can I have a paramedic please?'

———

Question: 'Julia, what does "minus" mean?'
Answer: 'It's them what's on strike, sir.'

———

I was listening to my grandson read a non-fiction book about dinosaurs and was explaining what the contents and the bibliography were for.

'Do you know what a glossary is, Damien?' I asked.

'Of course, granny, it's something shiny,' he replied.

———

A number of years ago when we used to have prayers in morning assembly, my nephew came home one day and asked his mum, 'Why do we say "old men" after our prayers?'

———

I asked my six-year-old granddaughter if she knew where her funny bone was.

'My teacher says,' she replied pertly, 'that a better word than funny to use is hilarious.'

———

When my children were young, one of them came to me with a broken toy and asked me to repair it. He said, 'Please mend my car. It has come from together.'

———

'There are five books in the Old Testament,' wrote a candidate in the RE examination, 'and the first begins with Guinness.'

———

friendly

Some years ago a small member of our family, aged five, could hardly wait to go to school. When she did, she loved it. When she heard they were going to 'break up' the school she was devastated. He mother consoled her and explained they were only 'breaking up' for a half-term holiday.

—

'And what position does your father play in the football team, Andrew?' asked an infant teacher. 'He plays drawback,' the child replied.

—

At the village Harvest Festival, my class were to sing 'The Lord of the Dance'. I had carefully chosen some children to sing individually the main lines and the rest of the class were to join in the chorus. All went well until it came to Gillian's turn. She was six years old and had a beautifully loud, clear voice. Just before our turn started, I asked them if they all knew the words. Gillian looked doubtful, so I printed them out for her on a piece of paper. She was to sing 'I was cold, I was naked, were you there, were you there?' I could see her looking at the paper, and she turned, smiled at me and sang in that lovely voice: 'I was cold, I was knackered, were you there, were you there?'

—

'My granny has had go to into hospital for an operation,' the small girl told her teacher, 'because she's misplaced her hip.'

—

'My daddy came in late last night,' the small boy told his teacher. 'My mum said he was as drunk as a skunk, and this morning he has a gangover.'

—

Carol, my three-year-old daughter, began crying in the middle of the night. I went to investigate and found her holding her hand over one ear, indicating that she was in a great deal of pain. She looked up at me and said, 'Mummy, I've got dire ear.'

———

'We're doing a play at school,' my daughter announced. 'I'm playing a rabbit and Daisy is playing the main part.'

'That's nice,' I told. 'What part is Daisy playing?' I asked.

'Alison.'

'I don't think I know that play,' I said.

'Course you do mummy,' replied Rebecca. 'It's Alison Wonderland.'

———

My four-year-old daughter Suzanne was in the car with me when I collected my other daughter Wendy from secondary school.

'What have you been up to today sweetheart?' I asked Wendy.

'I'm not telling in front of big ears,' Wendy said.

'Why can't I know? I always tell you what I do at school,' said Suzanne.

'Let's have a truce until after tea shall we?' I said as I got out of the car to go to the shops. As I got back into the car a few minutes later, Suzanne said: 'I know what Wendy learned in class today, mum'.

'Oh, really?'

'Yes, she's been talking about Queen Victoria's vagina.'

As I narrowly avoided crashing the car, Wendy shouted: 'I said Queen Victoria regina!'

———

'Girls should get married and boys shouldn't'

Love and Marriage

Despite his background, Barry was a remarkably cheerful little boy who never complained and always tried his limited best at his schoolwork.

He loved nothing better than straightening the chairs, collecting the books and tidying up the classroom. He took on all these tasks cheerfully, whistling away as if he hadn't a care in the world.

Barry's teacher was to get married over the Easter holiday and, before the last lesson of the term, the children in her class presented her with presents and cards, bunches of daffodils, tulips and other spring flowers.

Barry held back until the last. He was carrying two small branches of faded broom which had seen better days and a couple of forlorn irises, wrapped in a piece of colourful paper torn out of a magazine.

'I don't want you getting married. I don't want you to,' he told his teacher. 'I don't, I don't!' And he burst into tears.

'I'll still be the same person, Barry,' his teacher assured him. 'I won't be any different.'

'You will! You will!' he wailed piteously. 'I know you will.' Then he looked up, sniffing and rubbing his eyes. 'I wanted to marry you.'

The teacher wrapped her arms around his small, shaking body. 'And are these lovely flowers for me?' she asked.

'Yes, miss,' murmured the child.

'They're beautiful – these shall be my very special flowers.' Then she whispered: 'Thank you so much, Barry. I like them better than any other flowers I have been given.'

First Love

Kimberley Bloomer wore sensible shoes
And a bright pink cardigan and snow-white socks.
Her hair was gathered in bunches and tied with red ribbons.
When she stared at me with those big blue eyes
I went wobbly at the knees.

Kimberley Bloomer was the best reader in the class.
Her voice was as soft as the summer night
And her smile made me tremble.
I sat next to her for two days,
And she smelt of flowers and lavender soap.

Kimberley Bloomer helped me with my writing.
I remember her long fingers
With nails like pink seashells.
When I got things wrong she sighed,
And I felt funny deep inside.

Kimberley Bloomer moved away.
I never saw her again.
All year I ached for Kimberley Bloomer.

When asked by my small grandson why I have been married to grandpa for over fifty years, I told him that I loved grandpa and that he loved me, and that a long time ago we fell in love. Jack sighed. 'You know granny, I don't think I'm going to bother with this falling in love. It's like learning to do number work. It's too hard and it takes too long.'

—

I was giving my teenage granddaughter a bit of advice about boyfriends. 'Looks aren't everything, Debbie, you know.' I told her. 'Just so long as he's kind.'

'Oh, I know that, granny,' she replied. 'I'm looking for a boy who is kind of rich.'

—

There was a particularly graphic sex scene on the television when Toby, my eight-year-old grandson, came down to kiss me goodnight. I quickly reached for the set and turned it off. His sharp eyes had seen what had been on the screen. 'You really don't need to do that, granny,' he told me seriously. 'I'm not interested in that sort of thing just yet.'

—

At my cousin's wedding, one of the small bridesmaids asked the bride: 'After you've got married, will you have children?'

'I expect so,' replied the bride, smiling.

'And then will you get divorced?'

—

Nine year old to grandpa: 'I'm not rushing into getting married when I grow up. I'm finding school hard enough to cope with at the moment.'

—

'Before you get married,' announced my grandson Oliver, aged six, to his little friend, 'you should practise kissing. Girls like that sort of thing.'

—

Sebastian, my great-grandson, aged seven, was attending our diamond wedding celebration held at a hotel. Many of the speeches mentioned what a remarkable achievement it was for my husband and I to have been married for so many years.

Later Sebastian sidled up. 'I suppose you must have got a bit tired living with grandpa after all that time,' he remarked.

—

Joshua complained to me that 'the girls at school keep trying to kiss me in the playground. They chase me round and I don't like it.' Then he concluded: 'I think it must be something to do with the soap I use.'

—

'I'll never kiss a girl,' said my grandson Peter, aged nine, 'because if you do you have to marry her and have babies, and I'm too young for all that sort of thing.'

—

'All the girls in my class want to go out with me,' said my grandson Matthew, aged ten.

'Really?' I replied, very amused.

'I suppose it's one of the problems with being so handsome, granny.' He gave a heaving sigh. 'And I shall just have to put up with it.'

—

One morning at the breakfast table, my son shared his wisdom with us: 'Being in love is telling your wife that she looks really pretty when she doesn't.'

—

Our young daughters were discussing their futures, and the subject of weddings came up.

The elder said, 'And I'll be all in white from head to foot.'

The younger said, 'Oh, but you can't do that. You have to have "something blue".'

Her sister replied, 'That's no problem. I shall be wearing my navy-blue gym knickers. You know how comfy they are.'

—

My son John, aged eight, was in a philosophic mood. 'You know I think girls should get married and boys shouldn't,' he told me when we were at the shops. 'Girls like soppy things like dolls and babies, and cooking and cleaning up after people, and they don't like football.'

—

My niece, aged six, a bridesmaid at my sister's wedding, was interested in what the vicar had to say at the nuptial service. She proudly announced later at the reception that she knew another name for marriage. 'It's called holy acrimony,' she announced.

—

'Polygamy is when you have more than one wife,' wrote my grandson in his homework book. 'Monotony is when you only have the one.'

—

The seventh commandment, according to my grandson, is: 'Thou shalt not admit adultery'.

Postscript

When our eldest son Richard informed us he had asked Nina to marry him, my wife and I were over the moon. I was asked to compose a special poem for their wedding – something heartfelt and poignant and, of course, I was only too pleased to oblige. I am sure that many readers will identify with the sentiments which I here express.

When I am Old!

When I'm old and I'm wrinkly, I shall not live alone
In a pensioner's flat or an old people's home,
Or take an apartment on some distant shore.
I'll move in with my son and my daughter-in-law.

I'll return all the joy that my son gave to me
When he sat as a child on his dear father's knee.
He will welcome me willingly into his home
When I'm old and I'm wrinkly and all on my own.

I'll spill coffee on the carpet, leave marks on the wall,
I'll stagger home drunk and be sick in the hall.
I'll sing really loudly and slam every door,
When I live with my son and my daughter-in-law.

I'll rise from my bed in the late afternoon,
Throw the sheets on the floor and mess up my room.
I'll play ear-splitting music well into the night,
Go down for a snack and leave on every light.

I'll rest my old feet on the new leather chairs.
I'll drape dirty underwear all down the stairs,
I'll talk to my friends for hours on the phone
When I live with my son in his lovely new home.

I'll come in from the garden with mud on my shoes,
Flop on the settee for my afternoon snooze,
Expect that my tea will be ready by four
When I live my son and my daughter-in-law.

I'll leave all the dishes piled up in the sink
And invite all my noisy friends round for a drink,
I'll grumble and mumble, I'll complain and I'll moan
When I'm old and I'm wrinkly and all on my own.

I'll watch television hour after hour,
I'll not flush the toilet or wash out the shower
Oh, bliss, what a future for me is in store
When I move in with my son and my daughter-in-law.